MASTERPIECES BY
Michelangelo

MASTERPIECES BY
Michelangelo

BY JOHN CANADAY

AN **Artabras** BOOK

CROWN PUBLISHERS, INC. • NEW YORK, N.Y.

FRONT COVER
Last Judgment, **detail**
Commentary on page 106

FACING THE TITLE PAGE
Sistine Chapel
Commentary on page 107

ON THE TITLE PAGE
Michelangelo, **drawn by Giorgio Vasari**
and engraved by Christoforo Corillano

BACK COVER
David, **detail**
Commentary on page 107

Studies for the *Libyan Sibyl* furnished by
The Metropolitan Museum of Art.

All other photographs furnished by
Scala/Editorial Photocolor Archives, Inc.

Library of Congress Catalog Card Number: 79-54876
ISBN: 0-517-28748 X

CONTENTS

AUTHOR'S PREFACE

MICHELANGELO has been the subject of innumerable scholarly studies, textbook resumés, and biographies ranging from studiously respectful to outrageously romanticized. The purpose of this book is not to add one more item to any of these categories, but to supply through a selection of works with some close-range details an introduction to the nature of the genius of a man whose art—as the continuous flow of books about it proves—is inexhaustible. For facts, figures, and major accepted conjectures, I have drawn freely from numerous sources, as must anyone who writes about Michelangelo. Where I have disagreed, I have modified standard esthetic evaluations and added conjectures in the light of personal responses to the paintings and sculptures themselves, thus arriving at conclusions now and then that will surely seem heretical to the hierarchy of Michelangelo specialists. But in the end, the joy of art is the response between artist and observer, and if anything written here helps to stimulate that response in a reader, this book has been worth publishing.

For anyone interested in making a more thorough conquest of the subject, Howard Hibbard's *Michelangelo: Painter, Sculptor, Architect* as republished in 1978 with prodigal illustrations is suggested (The Vendome Press, distributed by the Viking Press) as are Frederick Hartt's *Michelangelo: Paintings* and *Michelangelo: The Complete Sculpture* published by Harry N. Abrams Inc. The mammoth *The Complete Works of Michelangelo* republished in 1965 by Reynal and Co., in association with William Morrow and Co. (An Artabras Book republished in 1978), is the most exhaustively illustrated of all books on the subject, with texts nearly as exhaustive by ten scholars who divided Michelangelo's painting, sculpture, architecture, and writings among themselves. And, of course, there are always the cities of Rome and Florence, where Michelangelo himself, immortal, still lives.

INTRODUCTION

MICHELANGELO. No other name in the history of art calls up so many superlatives. No other comes quite as close to justifying the superlative of superlatives—the greatest artist of all time. If the question had to be debated, Michelangelo's closest rival for the title would probably be his fellow Florentine, older by twenty-five years, Leonardo da Vinci—but on a different scale of values. The scope of Leonardo's powers, ranging through philosophical speculation, scientific observation of natural phenomena, inventive engineering, and the theory and practice of the arts, has made him the standard personification of that superlative degree of intellect called genius. But the art he actually produced, unlike Michelangelo's, leaves unsatisfied the yearning for passionate expression that is part of the human condition.

To call any art or artist the "greatest" of all is dangerous, or pointless, for greatness takes multiple forms from one age to another. It would be absurd, for instance, to weigh the sculpture of pagan Greece against the sculpture of mystical Christianity in the Middle Ages. The contrasts in conception, with corresponding contrasts in style, are too extreme for comparison. Nevertheless, Michelangelo's supremacy as an individual in his own time or any other time can be defended on the basis that he fused harmoniously two fundamental aspects of art that are usually thought of as antithetical—the classical spirit, which purifies and sublimates the passions, and romanticism, which exalts their power, even their violence.

Classicism in its purest form is a distillation by which the chaotic material of human experience is clarified and put into order. Romanticism accepts the mysteries of that experience as insoluble, plays terror in counterpoint against serenity, passion against intellect, our vulnerability to time and chance against our efforts to define our place in the world. Artists in the classical tradition revere the triumph of clarity and order in the monuments of the ancient world. The romantic artist is more likely to be moved by the fact that these same monuments are in ruins—evidence that civilizations must decay and die, just as youth must pass, beauty must fade, grandeur must crumble. Passion, not order, is ultimately the sublime romantic experience; yearning, not fulfillment, is the great romantic theme.

Michelangelo's genius lay in his dual nature as a classicist and a romantic, which is to say, in his capacity to endow passion with nobility, or nobility with passion, depending on whether you want to regard him as a romantic spirit adapting himself to his classical heritage, or an innately classical intellect revivifying the ideal tradition in response to his own passionate and tragic experience of life.

If we are overworking the word "passion" here, it is because no other word will do to conjoin the contrasting sources of Michelangelo's conceptions—his sheer sensual, often sexual, and altogether personal adulation of the body, and a mysticism that explains the body's existence and the existence of the universe in terms of divine miracle. These are the dual themes of the vast harmony of the Sistine ceiling, which, without equivocation, must be called the greatest painting ever created. Confronted by this testament of genius, it is folly for any critic or art historian to attempt to classify Michelangelo as anything less than a universal artist of the human spirit in all its complexity and contradiction—its capacity for logical control in struggle with its vulnerability to the invincible surge of emotions, which, defying reason, still add their own richness to the quiet, durable rewards of orderly contemplation.

If there is a question as to the pertinence of arguing that one artist or another is the greatest of all, there can be no question whatsoever as to Michelangelo's supremacy in having produced the greatest volume of work at the highest level of quality in the widest variety of fields. In that combination of superlatives he remains unapproached. Many artists, particularly in his time and the following century, were proficient in painting, sculpture, and architecture. Michelangelo is unique as a creator who (even though he always insisted that he was first of all a sculptor) was not merely proficient as a painter, a sculptor, and an architect, but was supreme in each field, with the planning of urban areas as adjunct to his design of buildings. The word "versatile" with its connotations of mere facility is totally inadequate to describe him; he was triply a genius. And if he had never painted the Sistine ceiling and the Last Judgment on the chapel's end wall; if he had never carved a stone or designed the dome that dominates the city of Rome; if none of his other buildings had forecast the redirection of architecture—if he had achieved none of all that, he would still hold a firm position in the history of Italian poetry.

What accounts for genius? Where does it come from? There are literary families, musical families, families of painters and families of scientists, where talent is carried on more or less genetically and nurtured through exposure, opportunity, and training. But talent, even great talent, is one thing, genius another. Genius appears unexpectedly, even irrationally. Leonardo da Vinci was the illegitimate son of a respectable Florentine notary and a girl of humble origins about whom we know virtually nothing except that her name was Caterina. (She has been a delight to romantic biographers, who have always felt free to invent her.) Michelangelo was born into a family, the Buonarroti (and baptized Michelagnolo di Lodovico Buonarroti Simoni), that held a legitimate position as gentry but a rather weak one as minor Florentine nobility—a family so devoid of distinction that Michelangelo all his life was sensitive on the subject. As not-quite-patricians, the family objected to the boy's determination to become an artist, beating being one of his father's methods of dissuasion—and then, after his success, they became parasites on his fame and his purse.

Michelangelo became famous so early (in his middle twenties) and lived so long (eighty-nine years, from 1475 to 1564) that his life is unusually well documented by contemporary references. Giorgio Vasari, the first art historian, a generation younger than Michelangelo, heard stories, saw the work, and followed the life of the great man at close range. In 1550 he published a biography of Michelangelo along with others of artists living and dead, in his *Lives of the most excellent painters, sculptors, and architects.* What he wrote about Michelangelo can hardly be called objective reporting in its idolization of *Il Divino*—The Divine One. Nor was Vasari ever too careful about checking the veracity of an interesting anecdote if it tied in with his own ideas of an artist's work and personality. His life of Michelangelo depended less on gossip and anecdotes of dubious authenticity than on his outlines of accounts of the lives of earlier artists that came down to him largely by hearsay. But even so, Michelangelo seems to have objected to parts of Vasari's story, and in 1553 he gave new material to one Ascanio Condivi for publication. Except for any fabrications that Michelangelo himself chose to include, and any incidents that he chose to omit, Condivi's account is a dependable one. Vasari borrowed from it in rewriting his *Lives* in 1568.

In addition to these major sources there are legal documents, various letters to or about Michelangelo and, above all, his own letters, written not for posterity but simply to meet the exigencies of a life that, far from being led in divine immunity from mundane matters, was beset from quarters low and high—from the nagging of his relatives to the importunities of popes. With all this material plus descriptions of his appearance and the moderately cosmeticized engraved portrait in Vasari's *Lives*, there is no possibility of visualizing Michelangelo as we often imagine other artists to have been —reflections of the images that they painted. It is no surprise to learn that Leonardo, the painter of lovely faces and graceful postures, was admired and sought after, in his youth, as much for his beauty as for his talent. The ideal image of Michelangelo would follow the pattern of God the Creator on the Sistine ceiling, and the sculptured Moses for the tomb of Julius II— both models of old age in vital splendor rather than in decay. We have, instead, the engraved record of a tortured face, its natural irregularities exaggerated by a nose so badly broken that it amounted to a severe deformity. Michelangelo was fourteen or fifteen years old when he suffered this disfigurement from the fist of a fellow student named Pietro Torrigiano who later boasted that "that fellow will carry my signature to his death." His version of the incident was that Michelangelo was in the habit of making fun of his fellow students' drawings, and that finally he, Torrigiano, lost his temper "more than usual" and delivered the blow, feeling the bone and cartilage crumple.

Michelangelo's spiritual autobiography is written in his paintings and sculptures and the most intimate of his poems. These self-revelatory sources have made him, like Leonardo, a rich subject for postmortem psychoanalysis. Conjectures as to a warped attachment to his mother, who died when he was a young boy, are, inevitably, basic to these twentieth-century reconstructions, especially since only one of her five sons ever married. Leaving psychoanalytical speculations aside for the moment, we are told that Michelangelo, sought after by popes and princes, with entrée to the highest intellectual circles in Florence and Rome, was careless and sometimes even slovenly in dress and attention to his person—not in the way of bohemian artists whose willful violation of social conventions is their earmark of a chosen way of life, but because the pressures and confusions that beset him left little time for the cultivation of superficial refinements. It is quite possible, also, that he rejected the idea of draping fine clothing upon a body that he despised, a rough, asymmetrical body that

tormented him with its sensuality, a sensuality that was repellent in an ugly body but noble when incarnated in the beautiful ones that Michelangelo carved, painted, and adored.

We are also told that Michelangelo was often touchy, quarrelsome, impatient, quick to take offense and quick to feel abused by criticism from his rivals—or would-be rivals, since the personal slanders and professional sniping aimed at him came from mean minds and small talents. Stung in spite of himself, he retorted like a giant swatting at flies. There must have been times in his life when he laughed, when he responded to a witticism or offered one in a less cryptic and bitter spirit than any that have come down to us. There must have been companionships, no matter how brief, that alleviated the harassment of self-doubt before Michelangelo found the relative appeasements of old age. Yet it is impossible to imagine Michelangelo relaxing over a drink with friends, as impossible to imagine him carousing as it is to visualize him suave and elegant at courtly affairs like those where his only rival in Rome, the handsome Raphael, shone so brilliantly.

As for liaisons or deep, enduring friendships during youth and middle age, surely these would have been put on record in one form or another, by friends or enemies, during the years when any bits of gossip or reminiscence about the old man who had become *Il Divino* were seized upon. The bully Torrigiano's account of his early claim to fame is one example. Benvenuto Cellini set it down in Torrigiano's words as he remembered them years later.

"Deep enduring friendships" do not include incidents like one we know from Michelangelo's letter and poems to a boy named Febo who quit as his studio assistant, apparently because of the great man's widespread reputation as a pederast. In a patient and affectionate letter Michelangelo rebukes Febo for listening to "other people's words, which you shouldn't believe since you have tested me," and says that he will always be at Febo's service "with faith and love." The letter expresses Michelangelo's hurt, and the tenderness he felt for the boy, with poignant dignity. An infatuated middle-aged lover abandoned by a pretty boy would have been more likely to grow recriminative in an effort to wound the boy as bitterly as the boy had wounded him.

"Since you have tested me" can hardly mean anything but that Febo had given Michelangelo every opportunity to declare his love sexually, without success. But "other people's words" followed Michelangelo to the grave. We know how scurrilous they could be by the example of Pietro Aretino, a brilliantly vicious satirist, adventurer, and blackmailer who wrote abusive works for hire. On the subject of Michelangelo's supposed homosexual practices, Aretino surpassed himself in malice after Michelangelo had failed to respond to Aretino's suggestion—a form of blackmail—that he would be happy to accept a drawing from the master's hand.

Opposed to such attacks, there are over-corrective efforts at the other extreme by historians and critics (beginning with Condivi) to represent Michelangelo as a man whose purity of soul could never have been tainted with homosexual yearnings, much less by homosexual activity. The question would be of no interest, or at least no relevance, in understanding Michelangelo's art except that he, of all artists, is the one whose most personal emotional life is all-pervasively reflected in his paintings and sculptures from early maturity through old age. Autobiographical interpretations can be made legitimately in many artists' work, sometimes with less probing than Michelangelo's requires. Rembrandt's self-portraits, as the most obvious instance, trace the course of his response to life from his ebullient, extroverted young manhood to his somber contemplation of the tragedy of old age. But no other artist has left us so intense and so consistent a spiritual autobiography as Michelangelo's, his lifelong efforts to come to terms with his God, to reconcile the glory of the body with the welfare of the soul, to free the intellect from the flesh and to be worthy, finally, of God's mercy.

It was not until his sixties that Michelangelo found the two loves that sustained him in his struggle, without entirely resolving it. One was a handsome young patrician named Tomasso de' Cavalieri, the other a rather plain middle-aged aristocratic widow, Vittoria Colonna. Both loves, within an elastic definition of the term, were Platonic.

Plato's *Symposium* propounds the poetic concept that the highest good is attained by the ascent of true lovers to eternal beauty. Everything here depends on the definition of "true lovers" as well as the abstractions "good" and "beauty." The idea has been distressingly abused, as has its extension—that what is good is always beautiful, and what is beautiful is always good.

Tomasso de' Cavalieri combined physical beauty with goodness in its moral sense and was endowed, into the bargain, with esthetic sensibility and a high degree of intelligence. Michelangelo's love for him is as noble an instance as can be found of sexual infatuation disciplined (if not quite exorcized) as "goodness" and "beauty." His letters to Cavalieri are philosophical love letters; his poems are love poems on elevated themes with only an occasional slip into expressions of physical desire. Cavalieri on his part revered the old man as a mentor and something close to a god; his letters are models of decorum, of deep love ennobled by restraint. The friendship endured for thirty-two years, from August, 1532, to Michelangelo's death, with Tomasso at his side, in 1564.

During his old age Michelangelo mellowed in his responses to potential friends, and they in turn were more tolerant of his defensive eccentricities. An exiled Florentine banker named Luigi del Riccio kept his affairs in order and received some poems in exchange. Vasari, too, received a poem with apologies for any shortcomings since "many say I am in my second childhood" and he "wanted to act the part." There were others, but only Vittoria Colonna's and Cavalieri's friendships reached his heart. They ran concurrently from 1536, when he met Vittoria Colonna, until her death in 1547.

Vittoria Colonna was distinguished not only by lineage but by the cultivation of an intellect respected by the foremost humanists of the day. No sublimations were necessary in this friendship devoid of any hint of sexual passion; in religious discussions with this pious, sensible, and fervently moral lady, Michelangelo found for the first time some purification of the sense of sin that had obsessed him for so long. For Cavalieri he created drawings on pagan subjects that could be translated into allegories of ideal love, but for Vittoria Colonna he chose the Crucifixion, Pietàs, obsessed now with the approach of his own death and hopes for salvation. Enfeebled toward the end, he worked at carving a Pietà (Page 101) that—rough, unfinished, and haunting—is part prayer and part answer.

J. C.

MASTERPIECES BY
Michelangelo

Sistine Chapel, Ceiling

THE VAULTED CEILING THAT confronted Michelangelo in 1508 when, reluctantly, he began the task of redecorating it, had been painted solid blue studded with golden stars, a standard treatment inherited from the Middle Ages and adaptable to ceilings flat or vaulted, large or small. The height and the area of the Sistine ceiling made it impractical for pictorial treatment—as visitors craning their necks to see it still know today. But insofar as the difficulties could be dealt with, Michelangelo disguised them with a scheme that divided the great stretch of uneventful surface into an illusionistically painted architectural composition that would remain one of the great tour-de-force decorative schemes of the Italian Renaissance even without the pictorial drama for which it supplies skeleton divisions.

To begin with, the vault is separated into transverse sections by ten painted ribs in positions determined by the actual architecture of the windowed wall from which they rise. Two long moldings (again illusionistic) running nearly the length of the ceiling define nine rectangular units of a size to enclose self-contained episodes of the biblical narrative.

This division of a ceiling into narrative units is an obvious solution and one that had been employed in numbers of other (although smaller) vaults over and again, but never before with such ingenuity. And from that point on, Michelangelo's ingenuity increases. He avoided the monotony inherent in episodic divisions of uniform size by alternating larger and smaller pictorial areas along the summit of the vault, tracing the story of the Creation; the Fall; the Flood, which destroyed the sinful and gave Noah, as a kind of second Adam, the opportunity to begin afresh in a world freed from sin; and finally the drunkenness of Noah, which, as a second and less majestic Fall, proved once more that in his frailty man must have an intermediary before God.

On either side of this central band, Hebrew prophets who foresaw the coming of a Messiah are ranged alternately with figures of the sibyls of pagan antiquity, whose cryptic sayings had been interpreted by theologians as holding prophecies of the same kind. A third range on each side is composed of small lunettes celebrating the legendary ancestors of Christ, with four large spandrels in the corners illustrating appropriate scenes from the Apocrypha.

In addition, bearing no apparent relationship to the story or to the figures of prophets and sibyls that they flank, twenty nude male figures (in Italian, *ignudi*) are seated on low square pedestals surmounting projections of the moldings. Their forebears, if they can be said to have any, would be sculptured allegorical figures of the kind often employed in architectural decoration, but these are youths of flesh and blood, Michelangelo's most fervent tribute to the beauty of the human body.

Creation of the Sun, Moon, and Vegetation

MICHELANGELO COMPRESSED THE story of Creation into five panels—the *Separation of Light from Darkness,* the *Creation of the Sun, Moon, and Vegetation,* the *Creation of Life in the Waters,* the *Creation of Adam,* and the *Creation of Eve.* The sun and moon were created on the fourth day, in the biblical account, vegetation on the third. Combining them in a single panel, Michelangelo originated an image unprecedented and still unsurpassed of the Creator, shown accompanied by angels as he hurtles towards us and across space, and again—in amazing foreshortening—continuing his course at such speed that in a moment he will vanish into the distance of the materializing universe.

Michelangelo achieved the contradictory feat of representing a solid figure of supernatural size propelled through the air not as if weightless, but charged with an energy that overcomes all obstacles without even being aware of them.

It is this conception of God as energy, and his works as its manifestation, that sets Michelangelo's image of the Creator apart from the well-preserved white-bearded patriarch envisioned by other artists. Arms widespread in a commanding gesture, he creates the sun and moon; a moment later, in response to his right hand lowered palm-down toward the earth, green life appears.

◀ OPEN PAGE

Creation of Adam

THE *CREATION OF ADAM* is the climactic episode in the story of Genesis as Michelangelo adapted it for the Sistine ceiling, the one on which he expended his creative energy to the utmost, and without question the one that has become most popular, and for the best reasons. The story is told with utmost clarity in forms as majestic as the event warrants. The languid Adam, beginning to lift himself from the earth as the first pulse of life stirs within the heavy muscles, can barely lift his hand to receive the charge of vitality that in the next moment will flow from the Creator as their fingertips touch. The Creator is now accompanied not only by angels, but also by unborn souls nestled within the cloudlike cloak, perhaps the souls of Jesus and Mary.

The Sistine ceiling is as close to a superhuman work of art as has ever been created; its emotional power is so profound and its philosophical complications so absorbing that the feat of its physical materialization, the plain manual achievement of painting it, is usually lost sight of after a statement of wonderment that Michelangelo, virtually unaided, completed it in only four years. A difficulty that artists are more likely than historians to appreciate is that in the *Creation of Adam,* as an example, Michelangelo on his scaffolding, painting in strained positions within a few feet of the ceiling, could at no time see more than a small portion of an area peopled by gigantic figures, yet he maintained cohesive relationships of every detail to the whole, as if he were working on a scale as small as the one in which the fresco is reduced to miniature size on the page of a book as we see it here.

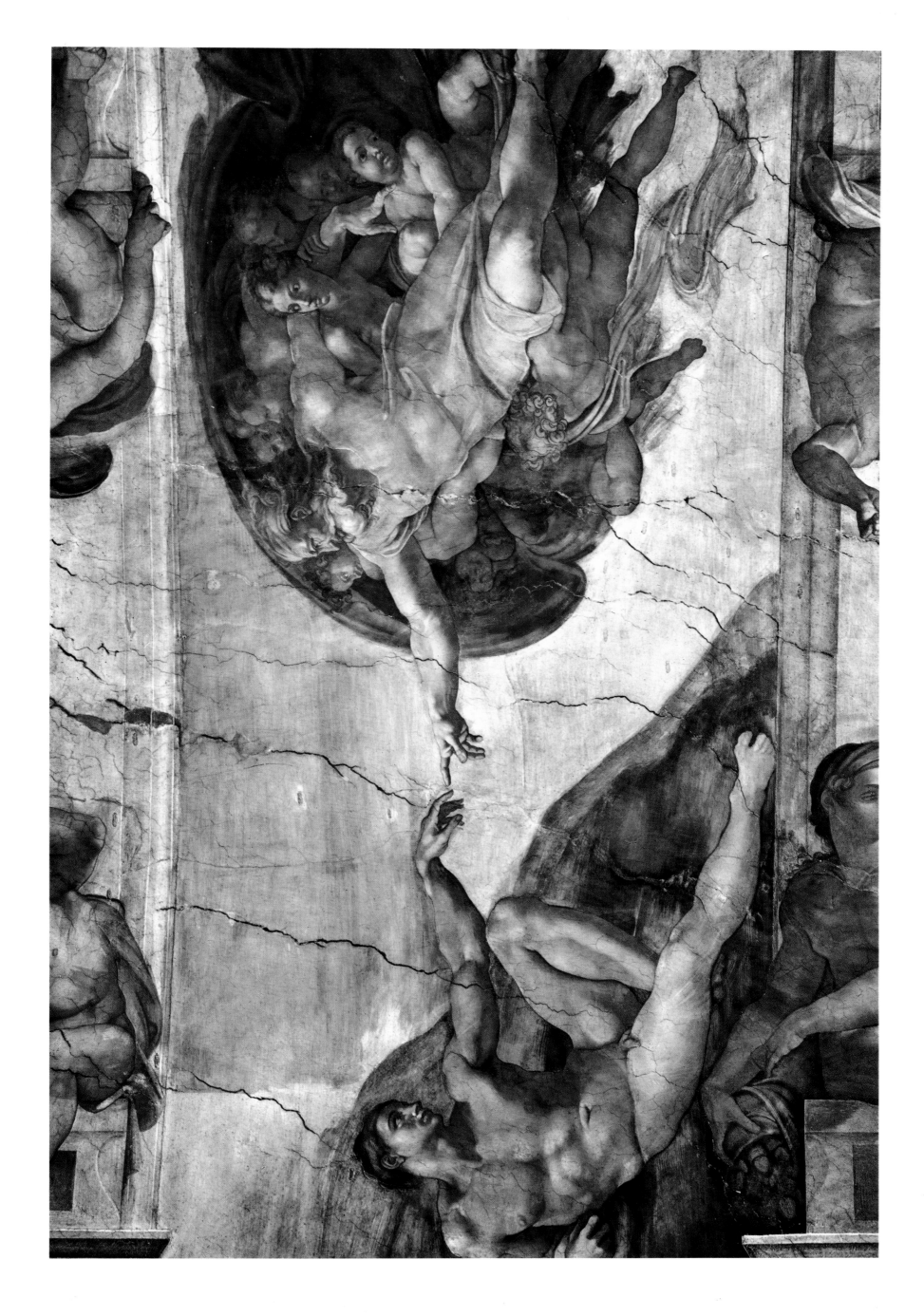

Creation of Adam

(DETAIL)

THE CREATION OF ADAM marks a dividing line in the progress of Michelangelo's decoration of the ceiling. He had accepted the assignment against his will at the insistence of Pope Julius II, interrupting work on another project, Julius's tomb, planned as a sculptured edifice of immense proportions. From the first, Michelangelo complained about the difficulty of painting the ceiling, insisting that painting "is not my profession. I lose my time fruitlessly. May God help me." (This in a letter to his father early in 1509.) In 1510, after months of virtually living on a platform atop scaffolding, he called his painting "dead" and himself "no painter" in a half-humorous, half-bitter sonnet describing himself as deformed by contortions demanded by painting a surface above his head— quite a different thing from painting a wall. His body was bent like a bow, he said; he had the breast of a Harpy, the back of his brain was relocated in his neck, which had developed a goiter; working with his beard pointing heavenward, his face made a "splendid floor" for paint dripping from his brush.

But as work progressed he became increasingly involved with the task as a rewarding creative effort rather than an imposition to be endured with the best skill he could muster. The Creation of Adam, painted in 1511, is both inspired and brilliantly calculated, the supreme masterpiece within the total marvel of the Sistine ceiling.

Creation of Adam

(DETAIL)

MICHELANGELO'S ADAM IS his apotheosis of the male body, the glorification of an ideal attained through a combination of self-discipline and intellectual rationalization. The guilts that tormented him as a sensualist are absolved in this languid, heroic, almost godlike image that ennobles the body without denying its erotic potential. The conception is close to the ancient Greek anthropomorphic ideal in which gods were given the bodies of athletes and victorious athletes could take on, for a day, something like godlike stature. When we call the Adam "Hellenic," we tie it to a tradition that, in fact, was known to Michelangelo only in coarsened echoes. The attitude and heroic quality of his Adam is close enough to the reclining figure called Herakles from the east pediment of the Parthenon to have been inspired by it, but during Michelangelo's lifetime the Parthenon sculptures were unknown in Europe even in copies. The ancient sculptures that Michelangelo knew and most admired, such as the *Laocoön* and the mighty *Belvedere Torso,* were late, melodramatic developments in the evolution of the classical tradition.

The difference between the conception of the Hellenic sculptures that Michelangelo's Adam recalls, and the conception of the Adam itself, is that the joys of the body were accepted in Greece as natural privileges of gods and men, and freely indulged, while Michelangelo, a devout Christian (unusually devout, for his century), suffered from an inbred mistrust of those joys. For that very reason, his idealization of the body makes up in romantic intensity what it lacks in true classical purity.

Creation of Adam

(DETAIL)

IN THE *CREATION OF ADAM* Michelangelo achieved the harmonious contradiction of fusing in a single image the concepts of God the Creator, most awesome of supernatural beings, and God the Father, a loving patriarch. The psychological relationship between Adam the son and God the Creator-Father is beautifully conceived and beautifully expressed in terms where tenderness is compatible with dignity, and awe with intimacy. As he stirs into life, Adam lifts his head toward the mighty figure hovering nearby. Both sight and consciousness are stirring at the moment preceding the instant of the life-giving touch of finger to finger; Adam looks into the face of God only half-comprehending what is taking place, and hence stricken by neither awe in the presence of the sublime, nor terror in the face of the supernatural. He responds, rather, with an instinctive filial love.

In composing the scene Michelangelo achieved yet another harmony of contradictions in unifying two halves of a picture that for expressive reasons had to be cut down the middle, dividing the earthly from the divine. The curve of Adam's body, with its echo in the reversed curve of the figure of God and his entourage, is the primary means of unification, but the climax of the episode—psychologically, compositionally, and as pure narration—comes in the two hands, in which the Creator's electric vitality is close to the instant of transmission to the still-languid Adam, whose hand can hardly lift itself from the wrist to receive the divine touch.

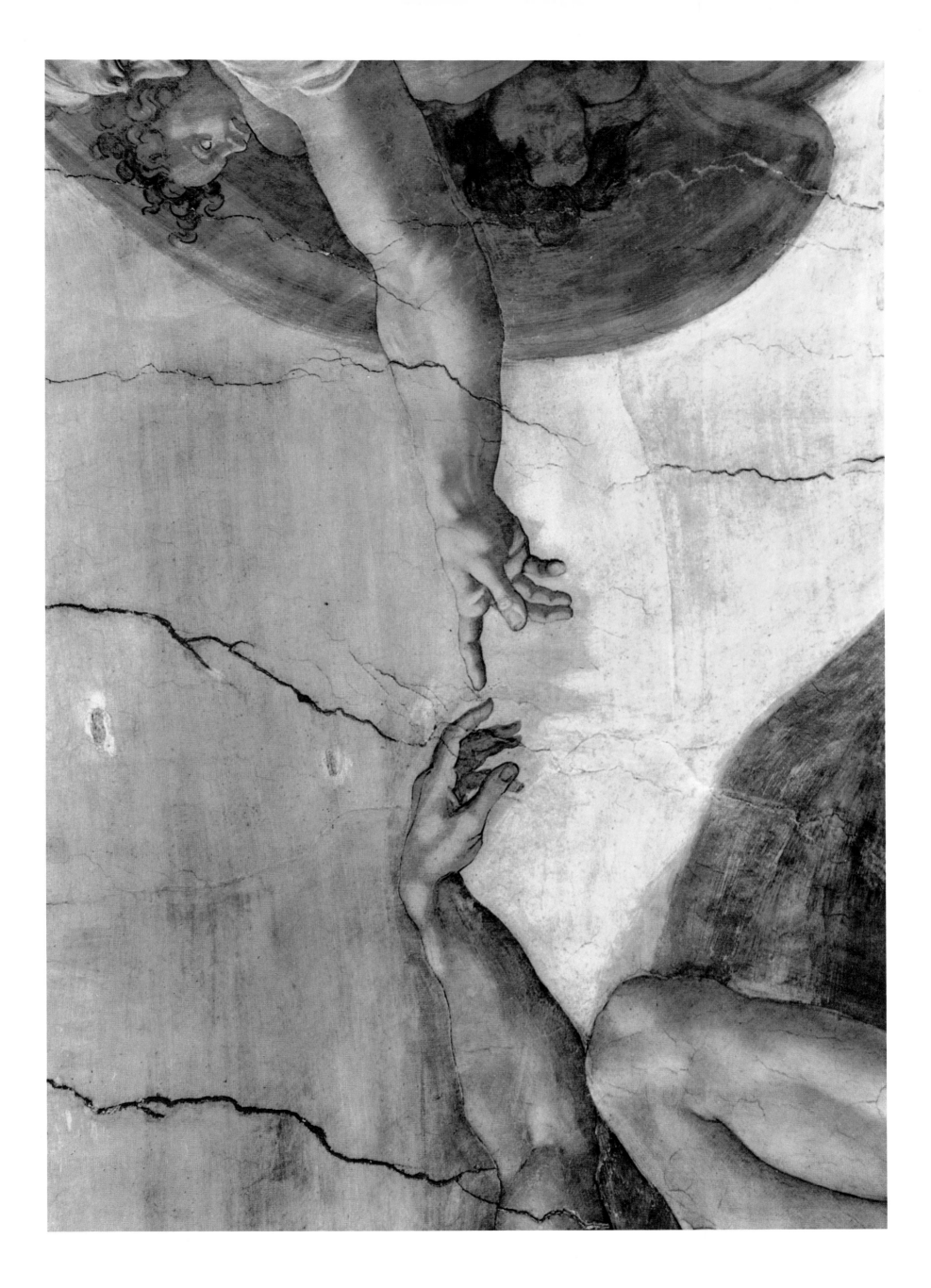

Creation of Eve

READING THE EPISODES chronologically, by which the *Creation of Eve* follows the *Creation of Adam*, it would appear that the Creator, who was at once so powerful and so benign in the *Creation of Adam*, has abandoned his celestial character and come down to earth to create a woman for Adam. But, as we will see later, Michelangelo painted the episodes in reverse order. This image of the Creator, the final one to appear in the narrative, was the first that Michelangelo painted. It must have dissatisfied Michelangelo, who thereafter conceived the much more impressive Creators in the other scenes.

In the *Creation of Eve* Michelangelo follows the conventional imagery by which God appears as a kind of master magician bringing sculpture to life. Even within that convention, however, Michelangelo's deity is supreme. The broad masses of the cloak suggest a figure even larger in proportion to the two human beings than it is in simple measurements; the idea of great size is emphasized also by deliberate crowding, requiring the Almighty to stoop in order to adapt his height to the picture area.

Iconologists point out that Eve often symbolizes the Church (and the Virgin Mary a second Eve) in the interlacing complexities of parallels, prophecies, and hidden cross-references by which medieval and early Renaissance theologians sought to rationalize the Old and New Testaments into an indissoluble whole. Eve as a symbol of the Church is an appropriate connection for a painting in the Sistine Chapel, although there may be a question as to whether or not this particular Eve, rising with almost animal-like obedience to God's commanding gesture, is endowed with the potential for so mighty a position.

Temptation and Expulsion

MICHELANGELO COMBINES THE *Temptation* and its sequel, the *Expulsion from Paradise,* in a two-part composition of such deceptive simplicity that its brilliance is likely to be overlooked. The tree of knowledge that divides the two parts of the story branches out on the left in luxuriant foliage over the Garden of Eden; its lines are echoed on the other side by the angel with his sword. Coiled around the tree, the iridescent serpent with the torso of a woman extends a hand with the fruit, which Eve is on the point of accepting. The horizontal curves of the serpent's arm and Adam's is repeated on the other side by the arm of the angel and, again, Adam's. The two halves are bound together also by the line of the horizon, which runs harsh and straight across the full length of the *Expulsion* but rises to a gentle curve seen for a moment in the distance of the earthly paradise.

These ties are obvious enough once they are noticed, but they do not answer the question as to why the scene on the left, occupying more than half the area and filled with eventful passages, does not overpower the *Expulsion* on the right, occupying less than half the space and devoid of anything but absolutely essential forms. It is a matter of "psychic balance," a modern term covering pictorial constructions that by all conventional rules should be out of balance, but in effect are as balanced as if they were symmetrical—and are more interesting for that reason.

In the case of the *Temptation and Expulsion*, the starkness of the wilderness, the emotional intensity of Adam and Eve expelled, hold our attention by their directness in contrast with the relatively complicated patterns of the *Temptation*. Nothing distracts from the anguish of the *Expulsion*.

Expulsion

(DETAIL)

MICHELANGELO'S ADAM AND EVE expelled are descended from innumerable repetitions of the subject in which the sinners cower in fear as they are driven from their lost Paradise by the Angel of the Lord. A little less than a century earlier (about 1425), Masaccio had given the formula new life in his frescoes in the Brancacci Chapel of the Church of the Carmine, where the naked man and woman are painted as real people suffering real emotions of shame rather than as puppets endowed with strained facial expressions. Michelangelo knew the frescoes, as every Florentine student did, and probably copied them, a routine assignment. (It was in that chapel, in fact, according to Torrigiano's report, that he, Michelangelo, made fun of the other students' drawings and received from Torrigiano the blow that broke his nose.) In his version on the Sistine ceiling Michelangelo might well have been paying conscious tribute to Masaccio—long dead—as his master by proxy. Inevitably, though, he extends and deepens the interpretation, contrasting the psychological reaction of the man and the woman. Adam's gesture is made in an agony of remorse and humiliation; he seems to raise his hands and turn his head away less in fear of the Angel than to spare himself the last sight of the Paradise he has forever sacrificed. He remains a noble figure in ruin, and hence a tragic one. Eve fares less well. Her young body has become thick and lumpy, her hair hangs in disarray, and her face is a harridan's. Symbolically, ugliness is identified with evil, and Michelangelo leaves no question as to where he places the guilt for the Fall.

Flood

THE *FLOOD* AND THE *Drunkenness of Noah*, the last episodes in the story told on the Sistine ceiling, were the first that Michelangelo painted. The scaffolding where he worked permitted only close-range vision; when it was removed and he saw his work from the floor, he discovered that he had not taken the distance of some sixty-five feet between floor and ceiling into account. In effect he had painted on the ceiling a scene designed to be viewed at normal distance on a wall, with the result that much of the detail is indecipherable from the floor. The shift to compositions in a few large masses like those so impressively disposed in the *Creation of Adam* was thus dictated by the practical consideration of visibility, but it also had the primary advantage of inspiring forms in harmony with the profundity of the subjects.

The scene of the Flood, which otherwise might have been conceived as a single terrifying manifestation of God's wrath, is broken into illustrative incidents something like an eyewitness report of a local disaster, and even these incidents are surprisingly ill-related to one another. The trouble with the *Flood* is not alone that of scale; the scene simply does not hang together. The major cohesive unit shows a hilltop in the foreground plane where desperate survivors are clambering to final and futile refuge. On the far right another bit of land, a stony crag, is crowded with men and women who have rigged up a makeshift shelter. Two of them reach out toward a muscular old man who carries an exhausted youth. The group is situated ambiguously in space; the old man appears to be standing on neither land nor water. In a third plane a fragile boat is on the point of foundering as struggling figures, now quite small, club others trying to climb aboard. In a fourth plane, diminutive figures man the Ark. It is impossible to argue that the four planes are convincingly related. Within the inconsistent assemblage of figures, however, there are pivotal ones—a young man who climbs the side of the rock with a woman on his back, the woman preceding him who clutches an infant in her arms—that express the terror and desperation that fail to come through in the scene as a whole.

Drunkenness of Noah

THE DRUNKENNESS OF NOAH is the second Fall of Man. The world was to have been purified of evil by the flood, but Noah, chosen as a second Adam and father of the race, soon demonstrated that the human spirit is irremediably frail and may be redeemed only through divine intervention. Michelangelo shows us the old man, discovered naked and drunken by his sons, a sorry spectacle but one that is deepened in meaning when the drunkenness is regarded symbolically as a violation of the spirit or, according to one Platonic interpretation, the imprisonment of the soul in the body.

Like the *Flood*, the *Drunkenness of Noah* tells better on the page of a book than it does on the ceiling, since its small scale and relatively complicated detail make it illegible from the floor. As a picture on a page it has —of all things—a certain graceful charm out of key with the rest of the ceiling. Noah resembles the river gods of Roman sculpture, and the sons—the one about to cover his father's nakedness with a cloak is in almost a dancing attitude—are modeled in low relief against a shallow background like an antique frieze. (A few restorations have been made following damages, but they seem to have been made judiciously.)

Our illustration includes the earliest of the nude male figures, or ignudi, which eventually were to number twenty. These early ones are notable for sheer decorative beauty rather than for the vitality that infuses later ones. It is also apparent from them that Michelangelo's original scheme was to pair the ignudi as reverse images of one another—the same pose reversed right and left, a device that, if continued through the ten pairs, would have become monotonous.

Ignudo

(ABOVE JEREMIAH AT LEFT)

IF MICHELANGELO OFFERED at any time an iconographical explanation for incorporating the ignudi into the scheme of the Sistine ceiling, there is no report of it. Speculative efforts to tie them other than decoratively to the prophets and sibyls below them or to the biblical scenes that they border, have come to nothing. The suggestion most frequently met is that they are angels—wingless, like all Michelangelo's angels—but there is little in their demeanor to support that idea. Any number of explanations could be synthesized from the infinite convolutions of neo-Platonic symbolism, with which Michelangelo had some acquaintance as a youth in Florence—but that would be nothing more than a game without rules.

It has also been suggested that in their masculine vitality these handsome nudes represent the unquenchable life force that began with the creation of Adam. But it is unlikely that Michelangelo would have had in mind an explanation that gave mankind's biological persistence a role of such prominence in a drama dedicated to divine miracle—at least not consciously. What is clear is that as work on the ceiling progressed, the purely decorative role of the ignudi, which we have just seen on the border of the *Drunkenness of Noah,* was expanded until, in spite of ambiguity, it rivaled the importance of the Creation scenes themselves. As the figures increase in size they also increase in variety of pose and vividness of personality, from the ideal Hellenic grace and repose of this ignudo (to the left above the Prophet Jeremiah) to others that have the feistiness of Roman street boys.

Ignudo

(ABOVE JEREMIAH AT RIGHT)

AMONG OTHER HOPEFUL CONJECTURES as to a unifying scheme for the ignudi, there is the one that as work progressed and the vast painting began to spread the length of the ceiling, Michelangelo's interest in the nudes as something more important than decorative accessories, increasing from figure to figure, led him to begin thinking of turning them into a catalogue of states of mind, or soul. The strongest hint that he might have considered something like a programmatic approach toward this end is found in the two ignudi above the Prophet Jeremiah, where the serene patrician youth on the left, that we have called "Hellenic," is paired in contrast with a more plebian figure on the right who bends under the weight of a garland carried across his shoulders—while his companion, freed of the burden, employs the garland casually as an armrest. The contrast is strong enough to justify the supposition that Michelangelo might have had some half-formulated symbolism in mind, but unfortunately there is no strong echo of the idea elsewhere.

The acorns clustered in the garlands here and elsewhere are a reference to the della Rovere family. "Rovere" in Italian means "oak," and both Sixtus IV, who built the Sistine Chapel, and Julius II, who decorated it, were della Roveres.

Ignudo

LACKING ANY STRONG EVIDENCE of a unifying scheme, symbolic or otherwise, for the ignudi, perhaps we can assume the pleasant likelihood that as Michelangelo labored at the titanic assignment he had accepted only under duress, the ignudi became for him a welcome relief at intervals between the demands of conceiving worthy expressions of the biblical theme to which he was committed. He can be imagined looking forward to the sheer pleasure of inventing variation after variation on the personal theme that remained always at the core of his life, his daemon, his worship of the body rationalized as a glorification of the Good in Platonic identification with Beauty. Without the ignudi— with their places on the ceiling occupied by twenty more decorous biblical personages —the Sistine ceiling would not be the consummate Renaissance monument that it is. That is, it would not be an expression of the fusion of pagan and Christian values by which those wonderful centuries lived in Italy.

Zechariah

SEVEN HEBREW PROPHETS WHO foresaw the coming of a Messiah and five pagan sibyls whose utterances or supposed utterances were similarily interpreted by Christian theologians are united, in Michelangelo's scheme, as previsioning the coming of Christ, which fulfilled the story of the Creation and the double Fall of Man told along the summit of the vault. Along the sides where the ceiling rises from the walls, five prophets alternate with five sibyls, with the two additional prophets—old Zechariah and young Jonah—assigned the most conspicuous positions, one above each end wall.

In the thirty-eighth book of the Old Testament, written at Jerusalem in 519–517 B.C., Zechariah recounts eight visions of the restitution of Israel and of a Messianic Kingdom, followed by prophecies of trouble and Jerusalem's eventual redemption. No vision of the coming of a Redeemer has been put more joyously than Zechariah's of the Messiah's entry into Jerusalem: "Rejoice greatly, O daughter of Zion; shout, O daughter of Jerusalem: behold, thy king cometh unto thee; he is just, and having salvation; lowly, and riding upon an ass, even upon a colt the foal of an ass . . . and he shall speak peace unto the nations: and his dominion shall be from sea to sea, and from the River to the ends of the earth." (9.9–10).

In its position over the entrance to the Sistine Chapel, the aged Zechariah was probably meant from the beginning to be played in contrast with the youthful Jonah as counterpart. The contrast was increased by the development of Michelangelo's style between the painting of Zechariah, the first of the prophets to be painted, and Jonah, in all likelihood the last. Zechariah is enthroned comfortably within an architectural framework that Michelangelo originally intended to repeat for each of the prophets and sibyls, but the confining elements have disappeared from the framework around Jonah (next illustration), a mighty youth who admits of no hampering accessories. Between the two prophets, over the four years in which he painted the ceiling, Michelangelo had developed the dynamic, muscular style that we think of as his most typical and most personal one, which would reach its explosive climax in the *Last Judgment*.

Jonah

JONAH, AS EVERYONE KNOWS, was thrown overboard where his presence had accounted for a storm at sea, and was swallowed by a monster of the deep (usually called a whale), to be vomited up alive on shore after three days. Christian interpretation makes the adventure of the Hebrew prophet a prefiguration of the death, entombment, and resurrection (after three days) of Christ. It might have been because Jonah is thus the prophet most intimately associated with the theme of the ceiling that Michelangelo assigned him the most conspicuous of the twelve positions occupied by prophets and sibyls—isolated from the others and centered directly above the altar. By the most fortunate of coincidences, the location established a close symbolical relationship with Christ the Judge when Michelangelo painted the Last Judgment on the end wall years later.

In its conspicuous position—and the only position on the ceiling that is really satisfactory as to visibility—the Jonah is a superb exhibition piece. It is unsurpassed (if equaled here and there) by any other of the prophets and sibyls in its dramatic pose, spectacular foreshortening, and decorative integration with a background that refers to the story. The head of a snouted water-creature at the right, and behind it a gentle angel, and finally a wind-tossed cherub, refer to the storm raised by divine powers after Jonah had boarded the ship in order to evade a command to preach reforms in Ninevah. Against these decoratively disposed allusions, Jonah, punished and miraculously given a second chance, looks heavenward in acceptance of the mission.

Jeremiah

ITS LENGTH— 118 FEET— makes the Sistine ceiling impossible to read as an entity, but the drama comes to its grand climax at the altar end of the room where Jonah, flanked on either side by Jeremiah and the Libyan Sibyl, surmounts the end wall with its Last Judgment—all visible as one stupendous unit.

The Libyan Sibyl and Jeremiah are the only two of the twelve prophets and sibyls who look downward; all the others either study their books or scrolls or look beyond and above them. With their quiet poses and gazing toward the altar— and toward us on the floor below—the Jeremiah and Libica are foils to the tempestuous Jonah, his torso and head thrown backward and to one side as he gazes upward in wild rapture.

Jeremiah, a preacher of moral reform in the seventh and sixth centuries B.C., interspersed his castigations, lamentations, and threats of doom with Messianic prophecies in which, as elsewhere in the Old Testament, the Messiah is referred to as the Branch of David. "Behold," wrote Jeremiah, "the days come, saith Jehovah, that I will raise unto David a righteous Branch, and he shall reign as king and deal wisely, and shall execute justice and righteousness in the land." (23:5)

The most obvious representation of Jeremiah would be a wrathful, woeful, or threatening figure. Michelangelo chose instead to show us a brooding patriarch. Contemplating the follies he looks down upon from his high place, pondering the human condition in all its frailty, the prophet is stirred not to action, moral preachment, or lamentation, but to melancholy.

Libyan Sibyl

THE *LIBYAN SIBYL* IS A RARITY in Michelangelo's art, either painting or sculpture— a major figure conceived in primarily decorative terms. By the amplitude of its forms and its schematic position this sibyl may take on by association certain humanistic virtues, but in itself it is a supremely ornamental figure that needs no other reason for being. It is tempting to believe that Michelangelo paired Jeremiah, the prophet of doom, opposite this serene sibyl in some kind of symbolical contrast of the poles of human temperament, but this would be presumptuous.

Analyzed in anything like terms of physical probability, the beautiful figure is absurd. The body is twisted from a profile view below the waist to a nearly full view at the shoulders. The head, in its turn, is drastically twisted on the neck. The thigh nearest us is unnaturally long, and the one in back even longer, which would leave the figure, if standing, with unmatched legs. In realistic terms there is hardly a rational proportion anywhere; the head is abnormally small even in the arbitrary terms of heroic sculpture, and the draperies of the robe and underskirt, as a minor inconsistency, have little to do with wearable garments; they are conceived as compositional masses only. But of course none of this makes any difference. If the attitude would be next to impossible of human assumption, it is easily and gracefully assumed by the Libyan Sibyl. Exquisite balances and rhythms are created from the raw material of mundane fact—which is always the privilege of art, toward whatever end.

Coloristically also the *Libyan Sibyl* is the most alluring of all Michelangelo's painted figures, contrasting with the stronger color and more resonant harmonies of some of the other sibyls, and with the appropriately more restrained, even somber, ones of, for instance, the *Jeremiah*. The color of the ceiling as a whole must have faded somewhat over the centuries and gives a first impression of a generally brownish tone, but when we focus on single areas, rich purples and greens, light blues, tawny orange-yellows, and brick reds emerge in rich orchestrations set off by accents of ivory whites.

LIBICA

Studies for the *Libyan Sibyl*

IF MICHELANGELO EVER MADE studies from a nude female model, there is no certain record of it. The model for the *Libyan Sibyl* is, as usual in his studies for female figures, male, to be modified by the addition of breasts, more generous hips, and more softening of musculature to feminize it. In any study, whether for male or female figures, Michelangelo described anatomical details—here, the muscles of the back and arms—in greater detail than he planned to use them; the study for Adam in the *Creation of Adam* was modified to emphasize only the most telling points of stress and relaxation, the twin aspects of functioning body-structure that invest an image with the quality of life and movement or potential movement. The pose of the *Libyan Sibyl* is pure invention; in this preliminary drawing Michelangelo made no effort to continue the figure in the almost impossible attitude of the complete painting. But the careful study of the left foot and, particularly, those of its big toe, show that from the first he had that peculiarly mannered pose in mind. The monumental volumes of the figure, lightened psychologically by the grace of the curving lines of the garments, spring from this toe; its tension, accepted without strain, is the genesis of an easy flow of support that comes finally to the heavy book—for which Michelangelo, on this sheet, included a study of the left hand.

The Metropolitan Museum of Art
Purchase, 1924, Joseph Pulitzer Bequest

Cumaean Sibyl

AT THE MIDPOINT OF THE ceiling Michelangelo placed a sibyl, a prophet, and a narrative episode—the *Creation of Eve*—that can be interrelated symbolically with more certainty than any other group. Both the *Cumaean Sibyl* and the *Ezekiel,* in facing positions at either side of the *Creation of Eve*, foresaw the Virgin Birth, while Eve is often a symbol, or forecast, of Mary.

In the case of the *Cumaean Sibyl* it was less necessary than usual for wishful theologians to fabricate a fitting prophecy; this priestess of Apollo was mentioned by Vergil in the *Fourth Eclogue* with a prediction that, since all sibyls spoke in riddles, could be interpreted to refer to Jesus in the guise of Apollo: "We have reached the last Era in Sibylline song. Time has conceived and the great Sequence of the Ages starts afresh. Justice, the Virgin, comes back to dwell with us, and the rule of Saturn is restored. The First born of the New Age is already on his way from high heaven down to earth. With him, the Iron Race shall end and Golden Man inherit all the world. Smile on the Baby's birth, Immaculate Lucina; your own Apollo is enthroned at last."

The cavern where the sibyl uttered her prophecies may still be visited in the ruins of ancient Cumae near Naples. As visualized by Michelangelo she is an ancient giantess so ponderous and so bent under her own weight that we feel she could shift position only with difficulty, even with pain, in spite of the powerful musculature revealed in the bare arm—an arm that Michelangelo would repeat some five years later in another giant, his sculptured *Moses*.

Ezekiel

EZEKIEL, AS MICHELANGELO'S counterpart to the Cumaean Sibyl, foretold the Virgin Birth in a passage reading, "Then he brought me back by the way of the outer gate of the sanctuary, which looketh toward the east; and it was shut. And Jehovah said unto me, This gate shall be shut; it shall not be opened, neither shall any man enter in by it; for Jehovah, the God of Israel, hath entered in by it; therefore it shall be shut. As for the prince, he shall sit therein as prince to eat bread before Jehovah; he shall enter by the way of the porch of the gate, and shall go out by the way of the same." (44.1–3.) The "gate" in Ezekiel's prophecy is a barrier to the sanctuary of Mary's womb. Michelangelo gave "gate" an additional reference by relating it to a barrier in the Sistine Chapel: the choir screen, now shifted to a different position, originally coincided on the floor with the band on the ceiling composed of the *Cumaean Sibyl,* the *Creation of Eve,* and *Ezekiel.*

In sequence with other prophets and sibyls in contemplative poses, Ezekiel is suddenly a figure stirred into action, as if in response to a message from the gesturing angel at our left—an exception among the figures accompanying the other prophets in that it participates directly in the action. In his left hand Ezekiel, who was both priest and prophet, holds a scroll that a moment ago he must have been studying; he has forgotten it in the electric moment of revelation, and turns away from it so suddenly that the scarves of his robes fly backward from his shoulders—in opposition to the stable sculptural masses below them. Whereas the preceding figures, beginning with Zechariah, sit easily within their architectural confines, Ezekiel's sudden action is held within the space only with difficulty. Michelangelo gave free play to subsequent figures, allowing them to project into space beyond the architectural scheme, often obscuring it, as we have seen in the *Jonah.*

EZECHIEL

Daniel

WITH FIVE POSITIONS TO BE filled along each side of the ceiling vault, and one at each end, making a total of twelve, the decision to fill those positions with figures of the twelve disciples was virtually automatic—and this was indeed the scheme initially agreed upon between Julius II and Michelangelo. About ten years earlier, Leonardo da Vinci had completed his famous *Last Supper* in Milan, combining everything known about the appearance of the individual disciples with his own exploration of their psychological characters. His translation of the sum of his researches and ponderings made his representations of the disciples the most impressive yet seen. Michelangelo was irrationally jealous of Leonardo, and one might conjecture, even if fruitlessly, how he might have gone about trying to surpass his rival. But the decision to fill the positions instead with alternate prophets and sibyls was a fortunate one, affording greater variety and (which was no doubt the determining consideration) incorporating antiquity into the Judeo-Christian matrix of the ceiling's theme.

Within the limitation of only seven characters, Michelangelo individualized his prophets within ranges running from youth to old age, from melancholy to ecstacy, from grandeur to intimacy. If Jonah is the most impressive member of the group, Daniel is surely the most engaging. Very young—hardly out of his teens and not old enough to have experienced the various adventures recorded in his book—he could be a student taking notes on a particularly interesting bit of research.

Last Judgment

Michelangelo was thirty-seven years old when he completed the Sistine ceiling in 1512. In 1536 he was called back to the Vatican to cover the chapel's end wall with a Last Judgment, the final episode in the story whose early chapters had concluded, on the ceiling, with the sibyls' and prophets' promise of a Redeemer.

In biblical history the promise had indeed been fulfilled; Christ had been born, had lived and taught, had been crucified, and died in expiation for men's sins. But in Michelangelo's experience, mankind had proven itself unworthy of the sacrifice. The twenty-four years that had passed between the completion of the ceiling and the beginning of work on the *Last Judgment* had been traumatic ones both for Rome and for Michelangelo personally. The city had been sacked by foreign troops who perpetrated horrors of murder, torture, and maiming on the populace. The Church was enfeebled with scandals at home and loss of dominions in the North; Michelangelo, an aging man at sixty-one, had been frustrated again and again until, perforce, the project that he had regarded as the core of his life, a gigantic sculptured tomb for Pope Julius II, had become his old man of the sea. He was beset by harrowing doubts as to his worthiness before his God, tormented by guilty knowledge of his obsessive sensuality. Faced by the world's venality, viciousness, corruption, and cruelty, and torn by the conflict within his own soul, Michelangelo must have felt that universal evils so outweighed such frailties as could be absolved, that damnation must be mankind's universal fate. In this mood he painted a Last Judgment so awesome that the Pope, Paul III, seeing it unveiled, is said to have fallen to his knees pleading to be spared judgment upon his sins.

The *Last Judgment* inspires various reactions, but the most usual one is that even the Blessed seem more tormented than blissful. By whatever interpretation, the vast painting is Michelangelo's ultimate tribute to the human body as the unparalleled vehicle for the expression of human emotion. In a torrent of flesh, nude bodies fly, strain, twist, bend, surge, and recoil in every attitude of shock, apprehension, terror, horror, suspense, and occasionally, hope or joy. Responding to the trumpeting of angels in the lower center, the dead at extreme lower left rise from their graves, initiating a spiraling upward movement toward the vortex of figures surrounding Christ. On the other side the torrent cascades downward, gaining momentum until, at the extreme lower right, the Damned writhe in their final agonies of despair. The black mouth of Hell toward which they are driven opens, in grim warning, above the chapel's High Altar.

Conversion of St. Paul

MICHELANGELO'S LAST PAINTINGS, begun late in 1542 when he was sixty-seven years old—thirty years after the completion of the Sistine ceiling and about a year and a half after the unveiling of the *Last Judgment*—come as puzzles. What has happened to the glorious breadth and clarity of the Creation scenes? To the passionate dramatics of the *Last Judgment*? To the pervasive lyrical images of male nudes? The *Conversion of St. Paul* and the *Crucifixion of St. Peter*, on facing walls of the Pauline Chapel in the Vatican, seem, by contrast with the earlier works, forbiddingly complex, strangely impersonal, enacted not by sentient beings but by figures of little beauty, too heavy to be marionettes yet animated by no will of their own. Among numerous scholarly studies, argumentative deductions, and provocative but questionable interpretations, we meet even the unsupportable contention that as products of Michelangelo's old age, the Pauline frescoes are simply evidence of failing powers.

The opposite is closer to the truth: the Pauline Chapel frescoes reflect a deliberate shift of direction in the old man's unflagging creative invention—the adoption of a more highly intellectualized, less emotionalized approach to the making of a painting. In the Creation scenes of the Sistine ceiling, and, even more, in the *Last Judgment*, we find impulsive or "inspirational" forces harmoniously interbred with such conventional disciplines as linear and formal interrelationships. But in the Pauline frescoes all impulse, all "inspiration," has not only been disciplined, but reduced to a minimum. Analysis overrides emotionalism, and the pagan sensuousness of the earlier paintings is totally rejected. If the Pauline frescoes are to be enjoyed, they have to be seen almost as if painted by another artist than the one who painted the Sistine ceiling and the *Last Judgment*.

Paul III, who had also commissioned the *Last Judgment*, probably worked with Michelangelo on the precise symbolism of the paintings for his new private chapel. The subjects are intimately related to himself as the incumbent pope in the first scene—the conversion of his namesake—and to the papacy as an institution in the second, for St. Peter was the first pope.

As Saul of Tarsus (his Jewish name), St. Paul was active in the persecution of Christianity. He was on his way to Damascus to help suppress Christianity there when a supernatural light struck him blind and the voice of Jesus reprimanded him. Led into Damascus, Saul was given shelter by Christians, regained his sight, and became the greatest of the missionary apostles.

"Companions" on the journey to Damascus are mentioned in the Bible, but not the entourage of retainers surrounding Saul in Michelangelo's account, which also introduces heavenly hosts. Saul was a young or middle-aged man at the time of his conversion; Michelangelo shows him old and bearded, as was Paul III—an obvious identification of the Apostle with the pope.

Crucifixion of St. Peter

CONDEMNED TO DEATH ON THE cross, St. Peter chose to be nailed to it upside down as an act of humility to avoid imitating Christ. Here even more than in the *Conversion of St. Paul,* Michelangelo shows the attendants in attitudes as if held in trance, more like automatons than human beings. The emotions legible in the masklike faces are formalized—almost diagrammatic—rather than spontaneous.

The shift from the intense emotionalism, the *terribilità*, of the *Last Judgment,* completed so short a time before, is less sudden than it seems. The *Last Judgment* was seven years in the painting, and Michelangelo followed a master design done in 1535. During those years, even though completing the *Last Judgment* according to the original conception, he had come to put more value on intellectualism and less on emotionalism as the source of faith—at least in art, which he described at this time as "a music and a melody that the intellect alone can understand, and that with difficulty." Howard Hibbard says of the *Crucifixion of St. Peter* that "the crucifiers seem to act out of divine necessity without malice or feeling, and the onlookers accept the martyrdom with resignation."

There are also practical reasons (if Michelangelo considered them) for the reserved, static composition partially realized in the first fresco and fully achieved in the second. The Pauline Chapel is a relatively small room with an intrusively elaborate scheme of sculptured architectural ornament. From a purely decorative point of view, murals of less effulgent character are a welcome relief, a harmony-by-contrast to the benefit of both architecture and painting. The Pauline frescoes may be works of Michelangelo's old age, but they reveal none of the illness, the fretfulness, and the obsession with the prospect of his own death that shortly began to change Michelangelo into a truly old man.

Madonna of the Steps

MICHELANGELO'S PAINTINGS, as we have now seen, were interspersed at wide intervals in a career that began in his teens and went on without interruption for more than seventy years until his death at the age of eighty-nine in 1564. It was a period of constant change in Italian art, with Michelangelo's own growth as a creative artist forecasting—and even generating—those changes. His story and the story of Italian art can be followed in a chronological survey of his sculptures.

Various dates have been given to the little *Madonna of the Steps,* but a very early one is most easily defended—possibly as early as 1490 when Michelangelo was only fifteen, which is not at all unreasonable in view of his precocious talent. He has followed the style of his first master-by-example, Donatello, the great sculptor of the fifteenth century, and has attempted, with a respectable degree of success to demonstrate proficiency in a technique invented by Donatello—*relievo schiacciato* or flattened relief. All low relief sculpture demands a consistent flattening of the third dimension of nature into a fraction of its true depth; *relievo schiacciato* is extremely difficult since the flattening, including distant objects, must be consistent within a depth only slightly raised above the back plane. Donatello went so far as to include landscape backgrounds in which the relief is so slight as to be imperceptible except in a raking light. Michelangelo, hardly less ambitious, attempts a stairway seen head-on receding in a room behind the Madonna, with figures in perspective. Daringly, he has turned the back of the Child toward us, and with equal daring but less success has tried to carve the Virgin's right foot in a foreshortened view from the ankle down. The figures in the background are unfinished, although their rough surfaces and vaguely defined forms give them, by happy chance, the hazy look of distant objects for which *relievo schiacciato* strives.

Donatello's most famous *schiacciato* relief (*Saint George and the Dragon*) was done about 1415. Michelangelo's one-man history of Italian Renaissance sculpture, then, begins with this Donatellian exercise, a backward look into a century that, by this time, was ending.

Bacchus

MICHELANGELO WAS NOT QUITE four months past his twenty-first birthday when Cardinal Raffaele Riario showed him through his collection of ancient statues and asked him whether he thought he could do as well—an interesting question from a collector of antiquities who had purchased as genuine a Cupid that Michelangelo had done in imitation of the antique. Michelangelo replied with a modesty that he perhaps did not feel, that he would do his best, and a block of marble was purchased. By some change of plan the statue was executed instead for the Cardinal's friend, Jacopo Galli, another (and more knowledgeable) collector of antiquities. Michelangelo produced for him a Bacchus that conformed to antique models in many ways—classical proportions, S-curved hipshot pose, and a proper set of accessories, such as the cup, the crown of vine leaves and grapes, and a leopard skin—the leopard being one of Bacchus's attributes. For good measure Michelangelo added a mischievous child-satyr at the base of the sculpture where structural support was needed.

But the *Bacchus* is not an exercise in classical imitation. It was a Bacchus such as had never before been seen. Bacchus was, after all, a god—the god of vegetation and fertility as well as of wine, and was represented in antiquity with a properly godlike body. Michelangelo's Bacchus is a soft-bodied, sly-faced youth of perverse beauty who, balanced a little uncertainly, leaning back from the waist, his head a bit wobbly, is obviously tipsy. In spite of its superficial classicism the *Bacchus* is realistic rather than ideal—the first sculpture in which Michelangelo's conception is his own rather than a demonstration of a prodigy's mastery of a current or antique mode. In context it is also evidence of versatility, for it was followed immediately by the profoundly spiritual *Pietà* in St. Peter's.

David

I<small>F A SINGLE</small> R<small>ENAISSANCE</small> sculpture or painting among the hundreds produced in Florence can be singled out as the symbol of that city in its greatest days, it would have to be Michelangelo's *David,* carved in the first four years of the sixteenth century—a precarious moment. With political troubles within the city and threats from powers outside it, Florence was, in fact, on the point of decline from the youthful vigor of the fifteenth century. But it was still a moment when an artist could produce in this David a summary of the vigor and that pride that Florentines held in the city's political and intellectual supremacy.

Contrary to traditional representations, Michelangelo's David is a youth in late adolescence on the verge of full manhood, rather than a young boy. We see him not after his victory, with the head of Goliath underfoot, but looking into the distance where Goliath will appear. The outsize hands and head are relics of the shifting proportions of adolescence, but otherwise the body is the lithe and perfectly proportioned one of a very young man—Michelangelo's ideal, even his fetish. Standing with one arm lowered, the hand holding a stone, the other bent at the elbow and raised, holding the sling over his shoulder, David is posed in contrapposto, the name given by the Italians to the balance of shifting weights that invests the representation of a figure with the quality of potential or imminent action even when in momentary repose. With the weight carried on the right leg, the pelvis is thrust upward; on the left, it is lowered and the leg is bent and relaxed, while in the torso the tensions are reversed. The head is turned at an angle to complete the series of counterbalances. Contrapposto is given more extreme expression in Michelangelo's later work—for instance, the *Jonah,* among others of the Sistine prophets and sibyls; the *David* does not go far beyond the traditional pose of classical standing sculptures. But it could never be mistaken for a classical sculpture, either in form or spirit. The body is not idealized or proportioned according to an established canon, as were Greek sculptures of gods and athletes, but is, rather, the perfect natural body of a young male. Nor is this young male either princely or ideally removed from life in the dreamlike serenity of the classical mood. Alert, vibrant, casting his eye in the distance where Goliath will appear, with a body beautifully muscled functionally, he is no Olympian, but a hero of the people, endowed, further, with the capacity for thought, an intellectual consciousness avoided by the Greeks in their formula of the ideal.

Pietà

THE SUBJECT OF THE *Pietà*, the Virgin holding the body of the dead Christ on her lap, occurred frequently in Northern painting and sculpture before Michelangelo gave it this, its most widely known and most beloved interpretation. Previous versions had stressed the grief of the Virgin Mother in more intense terms, sometimes (as in Germany) in terms of hysterical human anguish. Michelangelo stresses instead the divine aspects of a subject that is ultimately allegorical—the Virgin symbolizing the Church, and the body of Christ symbolizing the Eucharist, the sacrament by which the bread and wine of communion are the bread and wine of the Last Supper, of which Jesus told his disciples, "This is my body" and "This is my blood."

The symbolism, however, is lost on most observers; they see instead the beautiful gesture of the Virgin, by which she seems to tell us, as she gazes at the body, "See what they have done," while her personal grief is muted by knowledge of the transcendental significance of the Crucifixion. Nor do many people today seem to be troubled by the youthfulness of the Virgin, who, by any realistic measure, would have to have been a middle-aged woman. When this objection was raised by Michelangelo's contemporaries, he countered that youth and beauty are preserved by chastity, and that in the case of the Virgin, divine powers might also have had a hand in making her an exceptionally good example—a comment that, like numerous others that have come down to us from Michelangelo, might have been made less seriously than posterity has taken it.

He could also have pointed out that the symbolical nature of the subject justified the youthfulness of the Virgin; she need only be beautiful. And beautiful she is—the most beautiful woman by conventional standards that Michelangelo ever carved or painted. It might even be objected that in this *Pietà* both figures are too beautiful, that the appeal of the sculpture is primarily sensuous rather than spiritual. If this objection is made, however, it only puts this beautiful sculpture in line with the dominant trend of the older masters of the day, who capitalized on the same confusion of values.

In design and execution the *Pietà* is an astounding achievement, even if we forget that Michelangelo was twenty-five when he completed it. The irrational and awkward combination of the body of a grown man supported on the lap of a woman had always given trouble to both painters and sculptors, and rather more to sculptors than to painters, since the sheer incontrovertible physicality of stone or wood emphasized disparities that painters could to some extent gloss over. By a tour-de-force so perfect that it is hardly noticeable, Michelangelo supports the body on a massive lap that with its draperies takes on the strength of a catafalque, while the sheer beauty of the folds, which seem as much to rise from the floor as to fall from the knees, distracts us from the realization that the Virgin, if imagined standing, would be a grotesquely proportioned giantess.

Moses

AFTER THE FOUR-YEAR INTERRUPTION during which the man who described himself as "no painter" painted the Sistine ceiling, Michelangelo returned to sculpture. His *Moses* is the superb centerpiece of the sorry, patched-together vestige of a planned tomb for Julius II that was to have been the most grandiose architectural/sculptural structure of all time, dominating the interior of the world's largest building, St. Peter's, then under construction. Now tucked away in the small church of San Pietro in Vincoli, the *Moses* in its unimpressive setting is the conclusion of a story always told as "the tragedy of the tomb." Michelangelo from beginning to end thought of the tomb as the central project of his life (as much a monument to himself as to the pope), but Julius himself first interrupted work on it when he ordered Michelangelo to paint the Sistine ceiling. The rest of the story is a series of delays, modifications, and final defeat after Julius's death. No other pope could quite see the legitimacy of turning St. Peter's into a memorial chamber for Julius.

The *Moses* was to have occupied a corner position on the second story of the monument. In its present position on a shallow wall tomb, the statue is seen not only at close range from floor level but is crowded into a narrow alcove that imposes a frontal view. It was designed to be seen not only from below at a considerable distance, but at an angle, which explains the odd elongation of the torso and a sense of disconnection between the lower and upper parts as we now see them. These inconsistencies would have been corrected by foreshortening, which, Michelangelo said while carving the statue, he was calculating by eye rather than formula. (It has been suggested that he might have carved it lying on its back, which would give an opportunity in a large studio to approximate horizontally the vertical angle from which the statue would be seen in position.) From any point of view, physical or psychological, Michelangelo's *Moses* is a timeless symbol of vital intellectual force inspired by divine powers.

"Dying" and "Rebellious" Slaves

DURING THE FOUR YEARS when he was painting the Sistine ceiling, Michelangelo seems to have developed images that he might already have had in mind for development on Julius's tomb—among them the ignudi. The tomb was to have had at least forty sculptures, including a number of decorative male nudes adapted to symbolic or allegorical functions. Such functions have never been specifically discovered in the ceiling's ignudi, but in the variety of their physical attitudes they play upon the general theme of constraint and release, strain and repose, so that they are often accepted as symbolizing the soul's struggle to free itself from bondage to the flesh, and its yearning for redemption through grace.

So far as we can tell from Michelangelo's sketches and copies of them, the original scheme for the tomb was to have included figures of Victory on the lower level—direct allegories of the triumph of Christianity over Sin and Death—while figures comparable to the ignudi, but standing, would embellish pilasters that served as architectural divisions just as the ignudi embellish similar painted divisions on the ceiling. Two statues in the Louvre, very nearly completed, were certainly intended for that purpose. Long ago misnamed the "Dying Slave" and the "Rebellious Slave," their roles are closer to the reverse. The "dying" youth rises, with a languor similar to Adam's in the *Creation,* as if from sleep, bound only lightly with a band across his chest, with one hand raised as if to pluck at it. One feels that with full consciousness he will release himself easily. The "rebellious" figure seems rather to despair than to rebel against the bonds that tie him firmly, and he raises his head to implore mercy from a force more powerful than his body's.

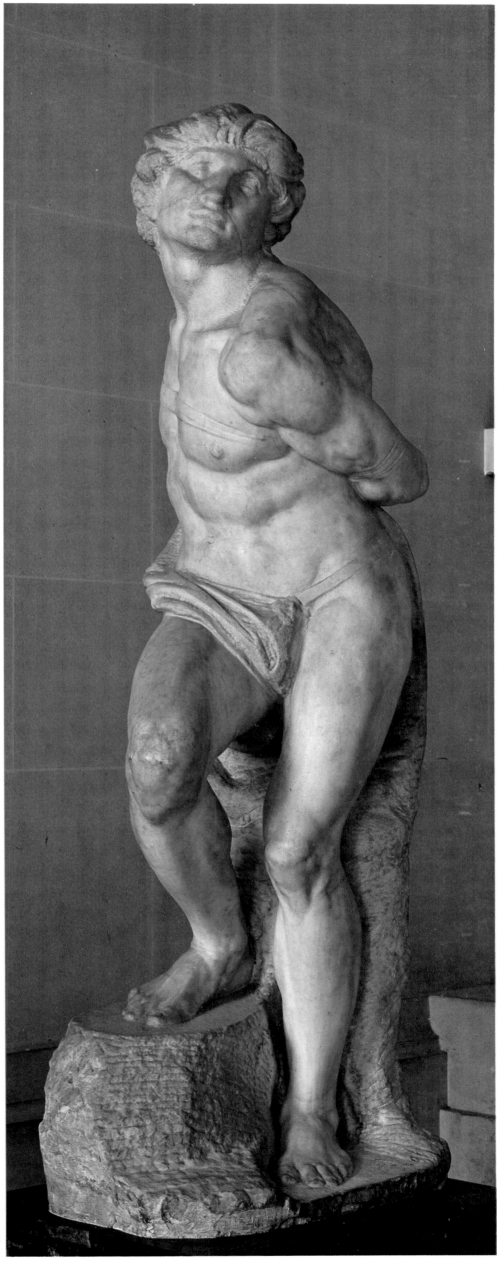

"Atlas" and "Awakening" Slave

AMONG OTHER SLAVES in varying stages of completion, the so-called *Atlas* and *Awakening Slave* are exceptionally arresting in their apparent agony as prisoners within stone, making them, by unintentional exaggeration, Michelangelo's most harrowing expression of the theme of the soul's struggle for release. The *Slaves* in general have been given numerous other interpretations, a credible one being that they represent the arts freed by Julius's patronage. Political interpretations have been suggested—the Church freed of any bondage to other powers. And from the most modern point of view, we might extend the idea to that of the release of pure energy from inert matter (which would bring us back to the Creation scenes where life, in the person of Adam, is created from insensate earth). It is not absurd, but rather another proof of the profundity of Michelangelo's art, to say that figures conceived in terms of the Church in the early sixteenth century can take on symbolical expression in terms of scientific discoveries in the twentieth.

In a context having nothing at all to do with Michelangelo's intentions, the *Slaves* have been important in modern art as examples of the sculptor's intimate association with his materials. Late in the nineteenth century Auguste Rodin, under the inspiration of the *Slaves,* deliberately modeled figures emerging from their materials as if delivered into life by the sculptor's hands. Twentieth-century artists, both sculptors and painters, extended the idea to the use of raw materials—straw, iron slag, scraps of cloth, bits of paper, including newspapers, among many other unconventional ones—without disguising them, reversing the age-long tradition by which the artist's function was to transform his materials into images of something else.

Tomb of Lorenzo de' Medici

THE DEATH OF JULIUS II only a year after the completion of the Sistine ceiling should have warned Michelangelo that any hopes that his tomb would be completed in monumental form had best be abandoned, but the project limped along through a series of reductive changes while Michelangelo went into the service of the Medici popes Leo X and Clement VII. Under their patronage he returned to Florence to design a funerary chapel for four Medici—Giuliano, duke of Nemours, and Lorenzo, duke of Urbino, mediocre princelings who had died young, and their distinguished forbears, for whom they had been named, Lorenzo the Magnificent and his murdered brother, Giuliano.

The chapel, added to the church of San Lorenzo and called, incorrectly but persistently, its New Sacristy, is Michelangelo's own architectural design. Originally it was to have sheltered a free-standing quadruple tomb. This idea was abandoned for a scheme of three wall tombs, two facing ones for the younger Medici and a double tomb on the wall between for the two elders, with an altar on the fourth wall.

The double tomb was never built, the sculpture for it is fragmentary, and the two wall tombs are incomplete and ill-related to the architectural scheme—but the chapel and its statues are Michelangelo's personal monument second only to the great ceiling.

Using Lorenzo's tomb as an illustration, we can try to approximate the intended schemes of the wall tombs—an elaborate allegory on time and man's fate. Close to floor level at each side of the sarcophagi there were to have been river gods (perhaps the four rivers of Hell) symbolizing time inchoate in the universe of brute matter. Resting on Lorenzo's sarcophagus are a male figure, Dusk, and a female, Dawn. (On Giuliano's, a male Day, and a female Night.) These represent time as measured by man—but time that eats away at man's days, his gradual murderer. The mortal remains in the sarcophagi are evidence of time's victory, but in the niche above, symbolical figures of the dukes (they are not portraits) represent man's victory over time, the victory of intelligence and the spirit over mortality. An elaborate iconographical superstructure fusing architecture, sculpture, and painting was gradually abandoned. What could have been the finest single interior of the Italian Renaissance ended as a rather spare and chilly shelter for Michelangelo's most evocative and disturbing sculptures.

As we have already seen in making conjectures about the Sistine ceiling, Michelangelo left art historians in a difficult position by making his own variations on conventional symbolism and providing no explanatory keys. Or perhaps it has been an advantage of sorts. Michelangelo's art is so evocative that it engenders multiple interpretations within the configurations of neo-Platonic philosophy; and within its humanistic breadth it inspires a variety of less specialized, and less precious, interpretations. The sculptures of the Medici Chapel have been Michelangelo's richest as sources for such speculations.

Tomb of Lorenzo de' Medici

(DETAIL)

BASIC TO MOST INTERPRETATIONS of the Medici statues is the assumption that they contrast the man of action, represented by Giuliano, with the man of thought, Lorenzo. There is the accompanying idea that Michelangelo, who had little respect for the two dukes (the son and grandson, respectively, of Lorenzo the Magnificent), thought of the statues as concealed tributes to more worthy members of the rapidly degenerating family. Lorenzo the Magnificent, Michelangelo's first sponsor, was a patron of the arts who even tried his hand at poetry; Michelangelo could have had this aspect of his personality in mind rather than that of the astute politician who ruled Florence during the climactic years of Medici power.

The thoughtful Lorenzo bears a superficial resemblance to the brooding Jeremiah of the Sistine ceiling, yet the differences are more important than the likenesses. The curiously bent wrist of Lorenzo's hand resting on one knee with the palm turned outward is an affectation in contrast wth the natural, relaxed position of Jeremiah's. The difference in the raised hand is slighter, but more important. The crook of the index finger, by which Jeremiah absently toys with a lock of his beard, is exaggerated in Lorenzo's hand, which calls on us to admire its fine design. Elegance pervades this figure, partly because it is elegantly costumed, but it would be elegant in pose and demeanor if nude.

Thinking back to the ceiling, the only figure that approaches this quality of elegance is the *Libyan Sibyl,* which we called primarily decorative, with its arbitrary pose and emphasis on ornamental details. The *Libica* forecasts one element of mannerism, an approach to art in which elegance was called into play as a substitute for the assurance, balance, and serene harmonies of the High Renaissance. Mannerism is the art of a moment of crisis following the brief years of fulfillment that found expression in the art of Leonardo, Raphael, and, until the Medici tombs, Michelangelo.

Michelangelo's own life was in crisis at this time; the della Rovere family nagged at him and threatened suit if their Julius's tomb were not completed; his republican sympathies were at odds with the despotism of the late Medici who were now his patrons; work on the tombs, interrupted time and again, went on from 1519 to 1534 until, in disgust and frustration, Michelangelo left Florence for the last time, with the statues for the tombs, the majority of them unfinished, lying on the floor.

Michelangelo's personal troubles and confusions, expressed in the troubled figures of the Medici Chapel, were the genesis of early mannerism, which also reflected the troubles of a changed Italy.

Giuliano de' Medici

GIULIANO, CALLED THE MAN of action, may or may not have been just that in Michelangelo's scheme. The statue has been interpreted as symbolizing Vigilance; less flatteringly, as Pride. Some iconologists have seen it as combining two of the four temperaments formulated by medieval physiologists, the sanguine and the choleric, which would leave the phlegmatic and melancholic for Lorenzo, appropriately enough. Without regard to specific symbolism, most historians have seen the Giuliano as dynamic, alert; but others have commented on its languor—not the languor of the Adam or the "dying" slave, which is a languor of potential vitality, but the languor of a muscular body overcome by inertia, unable to stir itself into action. As a very handsome and very young man, Lorenzo the Magnificent's brother Giuliano, murdered in his spectacular young manhood by political assassins, might have been Michelangelo's inspiration, disguised as a sculpture of his namesake.

Still, we may be exaggerating Michelangelo's contempt for the younger generation of Medici who are his nominal subjects. Giuliano, duke of Nemours, had the benefit of reflected glory during his lifetime. Michelangelo shows him holding a baton, symbol of his authority as a Captain of the Church, and holding a coin in his left hand, a tribute to his generosity as described by his contemporary, Baldassare Castiglione, in *The Courtier*, a treatise on etiquette, social problems, and intellectual exercises where Giuliano comes off very well.

Tomb of Lorenzo de' Medici

(DETAIL)

LORENZO AND GIULIANO ARE caparisoned in Roman ceremonial armor, a double reference identifying them both as Caesars and as Captains of the Church. Lorenzo's helmet, a wonderful piece of theatrical invention, is derived from a type worn by Etruscan warriors in sculptures Michelangelo must have known. But why is Lorenzo helmeted, while Giuliano is bareheaded? And not only helmeted, but posed in such a way that in the natural light of the chapel, by which the statue was meant to be seen, the face is thrown into shadow by the projection of the long bill, which in turn is the snout of a sinister lionlike beast? We can call on all kinds of associations here, inventing as we go. Is the beast, if a lion, a symbol of power, or of royalty, as it so often is? Or perhaps this head of a dead brute is in the nature of a trophy, the head of a dragon, symbol of evil, or any beast as the symbol of brute matter conquered by the intellect. If so, there is something inappropriate in its covering the skull of the thinker.

The shadowed face is generally accepted as appropriate when Lorenzo is thought of as the man of spiritual and intellectual contemplation. But in the contradictory interplay of neo-Platonic symbolism, shadow could also be identified with evil or the primitive darkness from which mankind arose—but this would refute the accepted theme of the sculptures. There is a final possibility: It could be that Michelangelo in the shadowed face referred to another kind of darkness, for Lorenzo de' Medici, duke of Urbino, died mad.

Dawn

WE HAVE MENTIONED ELEGANCE (plus a touch of affectation) as one general characteristic of mannerist art, suggesting that elegance or high style served as a kind of ornamental shell to conceal the spiritual void left in painting and sculpture after the moment of fulfillment called the High Renaissance could no longer be sustained. This, however, is only a partial explanation of the nature of mannerism. Minor painters and sculptors, of course, might follow the change of direction as a fashionable stylistic formula—"the latest thing"—but Michelangelo was never a fashionmonger. His personal insecurities and frustrations in the years when he was occupied with the Medici Chapel, paralleled in the life of the Church and the State by threats from abroad and uncertain leadership at home, were the genesis of the quality that makes mannerism an expression of its precarious moment in time. The mannerist mood is haunted by sinister forces that are sensed without being quite definable or, when definable, are invincible—forces that wait to strike, so that life becomes a day-to-day postponement of action even if action is possible. It is a mood of irresolution, frustration to the point of impotence, where, eventually, recourse to perverse beauties must serve as compensation for deeper satisfactions lost forever.

Michelangelo's mannerism stops short of this last stage, but the statues of the four times of day in the Medici Chapel are preeminently expressive of the mannerist mood of apprehension and frustration, of pain, anxiety, and exhaustion.

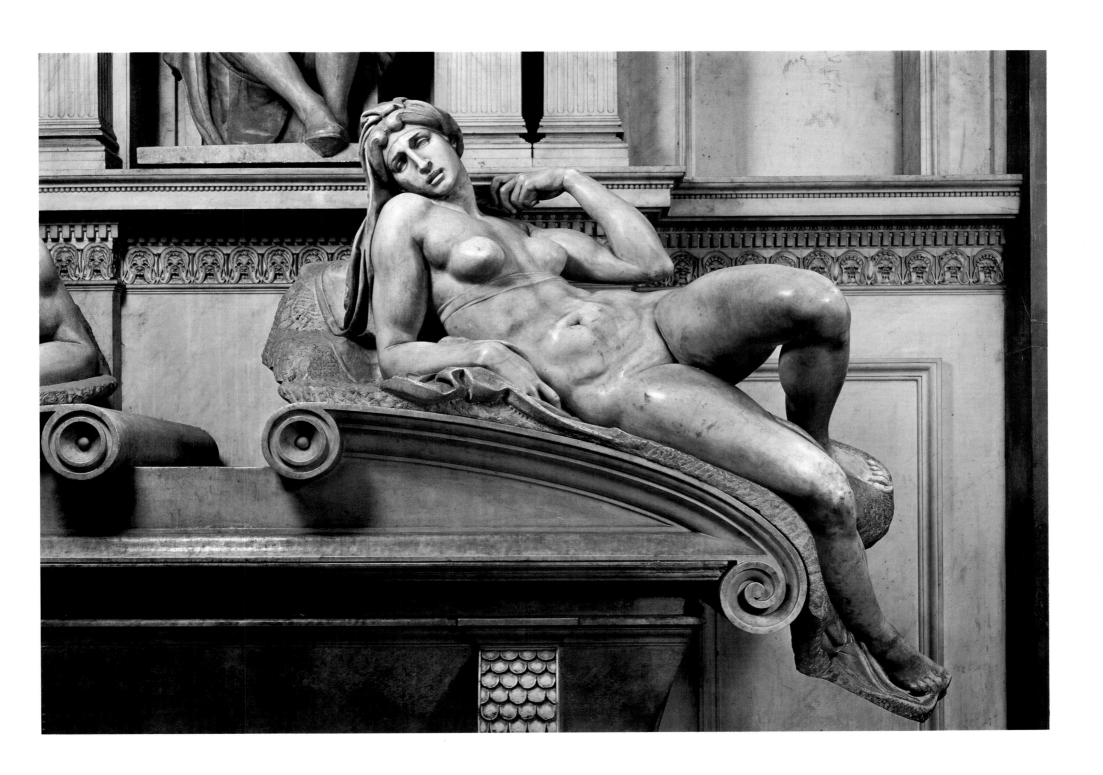

Dawn

(DETAIL)

DAWN HAS BEEN REPRESENTED in art as a babe greeting the sun with open arms; as the goddess Aurora bathed in light; as the god Apollo charging through the heavens in a glowing chariot; in any number of guises symbolizing renewal, fresh beginnings, and hope. Michelangelo's Dawn stirs into consciousness painfully, hardly able to lift her heavy limbs or to raise her head, reluctant to face full wakefulness, yet with no memory of the consolation of sleep. Like some of the *Slaves,* she is bound across the chest by a cincture, partaking of Michelangelo's persistent theme of constraint and release, tension and relaxation, but this time without hope of escape. Compare her with the Adam of the *Creation*—a figure equally heavy-limbed, equally languid, supporting his sagging weight on one elbow, his head lolling, an arm raised with effort just as Dawn's is crooked feebly toward a shoulder. But at the moment of half-consciousness the Adam is instinct with potential energy that, in *Dawn,* is already spent.

If the tables were turned—if Michelangelo had painted a Dawn for the Sistine ceiling and carved an Adam for the Medici Chapel—Dawn would have been a lambent Aurora, while Adam would have come to life reluctantly, with prescience of the unhappy fate in store for the race he would father.

Dusk

OF MICHELANGELO'S FOUR times of day, Dusk is the least pessimistically conceived. The body, once opulently muscled, is still sensuously beautiful in spite of the softening of age, and the attitude, for a moment, seems relaxed. But the right leg is crossed so curiously over the left thigh that it is uncomfortably strained, and even more than the *Dawn*, the sculpture as a whole is precariously balanced atop the sarcophagus, as if it might slip off. This positioning has never been satisfactorily explained, unless it was deliberately planned to emphasize the mood of unrest that so pervades all four of the sarcophagus statues. That the two on Lorenzo's sarcophagus were intended for the position is apparent because (unlike the other two, as we will see), their bases are carved to fit the curve of the lid. What we cannot tell is to what degree or in what way the figures of the river gods planned for the level below them might have engaged them more securely.

Even in that case, Dusk could never become a figure of rest at the end of day. The brooding head reflects upon the past with neither pleasure nor anguish, but with resignation tempered by regrets. Autobiographical references have been read into the sculpture—Michelangelo's own regret and resignation at this stage of his life when his troubles seemed to him to outweigh his accomplishments. The head could conceivably be an idealization of his own with its battered face, but it is not likely that Michelangelo would have chosen to attach it to so handsome a body, sensitive as he was to the ugliness of his own. Nor was his mood at this time of his life particularly resigned. By turns despondent and wrathful, he was vigorously alive, not for a moment resigned in the pursuit of his true life, his life as a creative artist.

Day

THE PESSIMISM OF THE Medici Chapel sculptures comes to full force, undiluted, in the figures of Day and Night on Giuliano's sarcophagus. The sinister quality of the unfinished *Day* is enhanced by its partial entrapment within the stone. The head, particularly, seems dehumanized by an evil enchantment that blocks its evolvement from base matter. But if finished and polished to the finest detail, the figure would still be entrapped by the pose in which Michelangelo has set it, an extreme contrapposto that frustrates its potential for movement. We have seen in other examples—the *Jonah* of the Sistine ceiling is one superb instance—that contrapposto, the shifting and turning and counterbalancing of the volumes of a figure in opposition to one another, is a device for investing a carved or painted body with the quality of action, of freedom of movement. Employing the same devices, Michelangelo reverses the usual function of contrapposto: The weight of one part of the body blocks rather than balances another. *Day* is a strongman robbed of the capacity for action. The most heavily muscled of Michelangelo's four figures, he turns as if to rise, strains to move but cannot, held within a terrifying dilemma that all of us have experienced in nightmare.

Night

VASARI CALLED MICHELANGELO'S *Night* the sculpture that would "blot out" not only other sculptors who hoped to surpass it, but, as well, any who hoped even to equal it. In answer to a verse praising the statue as one that would speak if it were awakened, Michelangelo, also in verse, called it a figure of forgetfulness, or at least of temporary oblivion much to be desired. "My sleep is sweet," he wrote, "but it is sweeter yet to be mere stone/In times when injustice and dishonor reign;/ To hear nothing, to feel nothing, is my good fortune/So do not wake me. Speak quietly."

Night is the only one of the statues of the times of day that is identified by traditional attributes—the star and crescent moon in the diadem, the nocturnal owl, and the poppy, flower of sleep. But in the usual wide range of interpretations, this *Night* has been called the symbol of both death and fecundity. The latter is more to the point, since this is a woman whose body bears evidence of the bearing and suckling of children. The owl, too, has been associated with the idea of birth by its location, as if just issued from the womb. The face of Night is untroubled, but the body is contorted into the most unreasonable, and least restful, of all the four figures, and the left arm is all but pulled out of its socket as it embraces a nightmarish mask.

Night

(DETAIL)

As if to deny any false suggestion that sleep can be even a temporary escape from evil—in spite of the verse he wrote later—Michelangelo cushioned his sleeping nude against a grotesque symbol, perhaps a symbol of death, more easily one of nightmare, and quite probably an incubus—the lascivious male demon who possesses mortal women in their sleep, and whose seed produces witches and deformed children. Michelangelo's prominent inclusion of this evil spirit with its black pits for eyes, its predatory mouth, its serpentine moustache, is surely more than a decorative conceit. As an enlightened man of the Renaissance, Michelangelo could hardly have believed in the medieval superstition of the incubus, but in the other direction of time, the twentieth century has deciphered symbolic meanings by subjecting Michelangelo to postmortem Freudian psychoanalysis. Given his fear of women, his feelings of guilt, and his efforts to purify his sexual yearnings by rationalizing them as a love of ideal beauty, it should not be surprising that he should conceive Night's lover as a fiend.

Florence Pietà

AT SOME TIME A FEW YEARS one side or the other of 1545, Michelangelo, feeling old and full of sin, began a sculpture combining the themes of the Descent from the Cross, the Pietà, and the Entombment, which he intended to be placed at his own grave. Late in 1555—he was now eighty years old—he abandoned the piece in partly finished condition and, according to Vasari, broke it to pieces, but was persuaded not to destroy it further. Christ's left arm has been patched together; his left leg, which would have been thrown across the Virgin's lap, is missing; the small female figure on our left, one of the three Marys, was finished, to its ruination, by a mediocre sculptor named Calcagni. Other parts had the better fortune to remain unfinished as Michelangelo left them, including the face of Nicodemus or Joseph at the apex of the triangular composition, which is generally accepted as Michelangelo's self-portrait. He seems to have abandoned the project for the double reason that the stone was too hard and brittle for his chisel (and perhaps for his failing strength) and that he was dissatisfied with what he had done.

In spite of disfigurements and partly because of rough passages (which appeal to modern taste), the *Florence Pietà*, as it is called, remains one of Michelangelo's most affecting works. It is also his most humble in spirit. At a time when tomb sculptures were oratorical glorifications of the achievements of the deceased, this one is a prayer—Michelangelo's plea, poignant and reverent, for acceptance by his God.

Rondanini Pietà

FOLLOWING THE ABANDONMENT of the *Florence Pietà,* Michelangelo returned to a standing Pietà begun many years earlier and began to recarve it, completely destroying the original image. Very old now, and enfeebled, he worked at the statue whenever he could from 1556 until six days before his death in 1564.

We may look at this crudely hacked piece of stone in either of two ways—as pathetic evidence of failed powers, which of course it is from any objective point of view, or as an intensely expressive sculpture for the very reason of its malformations. Schools of modern art that emphasize expressiveness at the cost of technical polish have taught us to respond to whatever emotive content is inherent—for us—in a work of art, whether or not our response agrees with what the artist was trying to put there. We have made our own interpretations of the art of savages, children, and the insane, interpretations that would surprise the artists. The modern movement called expressionism adapts such technical crudities to consciously directed emotive goals. Seen in this way, the poor, mangled piece of stone called the *Rondanini Pietà* is invested with an expressive force more personal and more intense than that of any of Michelangelo's finished sculptures, and allies him—no matter how arbitrarily—with the twentieth century.

Campidoglio

(CAPITOLINE HILL)

MICHELANGELO'S DESIGN FOR THE Campidoglio—the Capitoline Hill, which had been the capitol of ancient Rome—solved a problem that could have become a classic for students of architecture and urban design if Michelangelo had not reached its perfect solution in 1537. The problem:

Given: two existing buildings, one medieval, the other fifteenth-century (respectively, the Palazzo dei Senatori, or Palace of the Senators, and the Palazzo dei Conservatori, or Palace of the Conservators), forming an 80-degree angle on an elevated site surrounded by a mixture of other structures dating from antiquity to the present.

Required: to create a monumental plaza incorporating the two existing buildings, of such quality that the power of ancient Rome will be expressed as continuing in the present. (The problem was set by Pope Paul III, for whom Roman power in the Renaissance meant the power of the papacy.)

The immediate difficulty was the 80-degree angle. By all rules of urban plazas, the basis for the design would be a rectangular area, preferably square. Turning the difficulty into an advantage, Michelangelo mirrored the 80-degree angle by a third building opposite the Conservatori and left the fourth side open, thus making the Senatori the climactic building at the large end of a trapezoid that tapered toward the opening and a flight of steps leading up to it from the city. (Psychologically the steps lead up from the city rather than down from the plaza.) The pattern of the pavement was thus compressed from circular to oval—a form that had been avoided as unstable in Renaissance design, but became popular, henceforth, as a basis for the more dynamic baroque style, which set greater store on excitement than on stability. Again, Michelangelo was a prophet.

St. Peter's

MICHELANGELO TOOK OVER the redesigning and supervision of construction of St. Peter's in 1546, forty-one years after Bramante, the original architect, made his first plan. In the meanwhile the plan had passed through the hands of a number of architects, each of whom elaborated Bramante's scheme while the building remained unfinished. Bramante's plan was a Greek cross (that is, a cross with four equal arms) with a large central dome and four smaller ones, a clear, uncomplicated scheme that had all but disappeared within the snowflake complexities of subsequent variations. Very little building had been done during the years of proposed changes; Bramante's four enormous supports for the central dome had been standing so long that vines and shrubs were growing from them; they must have looked more like a ruin than a beginning when work was resumed under Michelangelo.

Instead of further elaborating the plan, Michelangelo not only swept away the elaborations but went further and simplified Bramante's scheme. As we now see the building, Michelangelo's St. Peter's is largely obscured by the lengthy nave, a later addition. But some idea of what he intended can be gained from a view toward the apse. A major change even here is that the dome, built after his death, was heightened above the drum, tapering with an effect of lightness contrary to Michelangelo's design of a hemisphere—which would have capped the scheme with a more weighty finality. Even so, the dome of St. Peter's, generally recognized as the most beautiful in the world, is Michelangelo's.

Last Judgment

(DETAIL)

MICHELANGELO'S CHRIST THE JUDGE follows an iconographical pattern dictated by centuries of use but varies it in startling and occasionally puzzling ways. Conventionally, Christ was represented with his right hand raised in blessing for those souls who will rise to heaven, and his left lowered to condemn the damned to hell. Yet both gestures are ambiguous here. Since Christ looks toward the bands of sinners, the raised arm seems more ready to smite than to bless, while the other, not entirely lowered, might be (according to some interpretations) hesitating at the moment before signaling the end of the world, its final destruction, or (according to others) pointing to the wound in Christ's side inflicted at the time of the Crucifixion, as if to remind men of their perfidy.

Conventionally, also, the robed Christ would have been seated within a mandorla, or aureole, an almond-shaped pattern surrounding the body of a person endowed with divine light—usually Christ or the Virgin. Michelangelo discarded this symbol and placed his Christ against a burst of sunlike radiance, which, in combination with the body's heroic nudity and beardless face, identifies Christ with the pagan Apollo, or Helios, the sun god. In addition to his other attributes (such as patronage of the arts, music, poetry, philosophy, and medicine) Apollo/Helios was an extremely moral god, associated with purification, law, and the meting out of justice. Thus regarded, Michelangelo's Hellenistic Christ is a hybrid of two sympathetic ideals and affirms the neo-Plantonic postulate, popular with Renaissance intellectuals, that the soul seeks mystical union with a single source from which all existence emanates.

Sistine Chapel

THE SISTINE CHAPEL IN THE Vatican, private chapel of the popes, was built in 1473 during the papacy of Sixtus IV and is named for him—but it belongs to Michelangelo. Devoid of architectural distinction, the vaulted barnlike room is easier to think of as the shelter of Michelangelo's paintings than as a building they were commissioned to decorate. There are earlier frescoes on the side walls expounding dual themes appropriate to the ruling Church—the theme of Law, symbolized by the life of Moses, and the theme of Grace, symbolized by the life of Christ. Although painted by Botticelli, Ghirlandaio, Perugino, Pinturicchio, artists, and other artists of sufficient eminence to have received the honor of papal command performances, the frescoes on the side walls are reduced to the level of estimable but somewhat dry narratives by the emotional and intellectual force of Michelangelo's ceiling and Last Judgment.

ON THE BACK COVER

David

(DETAIL)

THE INTELLECTUAL CONSCIOUSNESS, the intense concentration of the scowling brow and the almost fierce gaze of the eyes, so at odds with classical serenity, finally divorce Michelangelo's *David* from any classical prototypes in spite of the classical echo in its stance—a difference recognized by Michelangelo's contemporaries as a revolution in the history of sculpture. The point is not weakened by the fact that the scowl, the gaze, as we see them at close range, are accentuated by the deep undercutting of the hair and eyes, a technical exaggeration designed to make them visible from a distance.